Old TANDRAGEE, RICHHILL, MARKETHILL and POYNTZPASS
with LOUGHGALL, CLARE, LAURELVALE, GLENANNE, MU... ISBAWN

by
Alex F. Young, with photographs from the Des Q...

In this early twentieth century photograph by William John Napier, Tom Hampden the postman makes his way up Tandragee's Market Street, having passed the premises of Boyd Coburn the draper, George Dickson the grocer, John E. Maginnis the woollen draper and Graham's boot and shoe store. Born at Mullaghlass around 1870, Napier was a nineteen year old studying chemistry at Portadown Technical College when a diseased hip necessitated the amputation of a leg (it was buried where he was later laid to rest in Tandragee Presbyterian Churchyard) and ended a promising career. However, his interest in photography then blossomed into a full-time profession, supplying the increasing demand for postcard photographs across counties Down and Armagh. One idiosyncrasy separated him from other photographers. Where they signed or printed their names in a corner of their works, if at all, Napier's can be found on a gatepost, along a railway line or, as in this case, on the side of a cart. Falling ill with a kidney problem in 1914, he was taken to the hospital run by his sisters Margaret and Agnes in Lytham St Annes, Lancashire, where he died on the operating table. He was forty-nine years old.

Text © Alex F. Young, 2003.
First published in the United Kingdom, 2003,
by Stenlake Publishing,
Telephone / Fax: 01290 551122

ISBN 1 84033 244 1

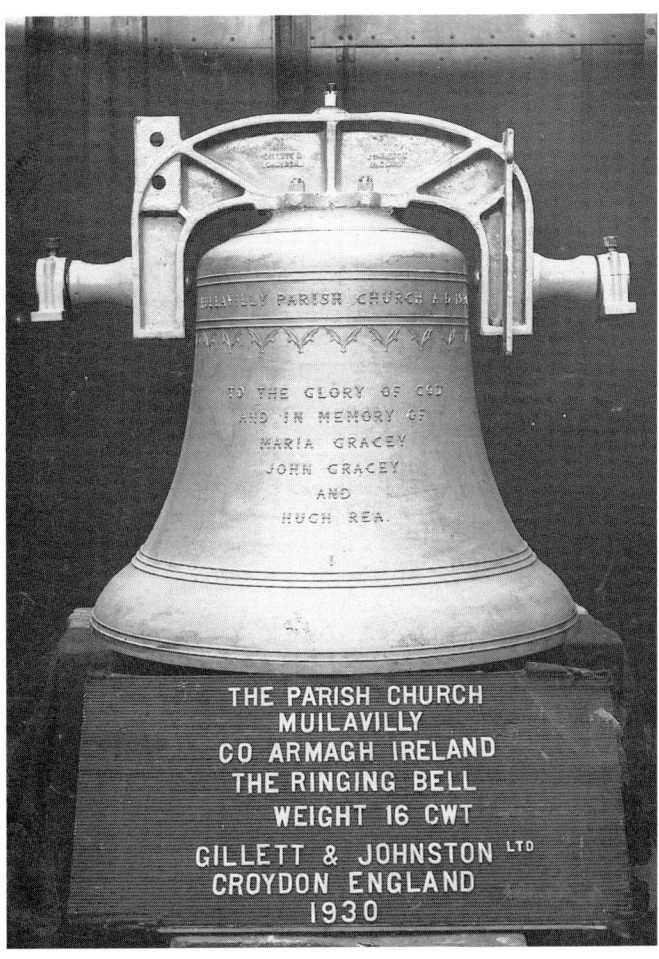

THE PUBLISHERS REGRET THAT THEY CANNOT SUPPLY
COPIES OF ANY PICTURES FEATURED IN THIS BOOK.

FURTHER READING

The books listed below were used by the author during his research. Only one is available from Stenlake Publishing. Those interested in finding out more are advised to contact their local bookshop or reference library.

Ordnance Survey Memoirs of Ireland, Parishes of County Armagh, 1835–8.
George Bassett, *The Book of County Armagh*, 1888.
Angelique Day and Patrick McWilliams, *The Institute of Irish Studies*, 1990.
Stephen Johnson, *Lost Railways of Co. Down and Co. Armagh*, Stenlake Publishing, 2002.
Mid-Armagh Community Network, *Dacent Fowk*, 2001.
J.R. Whitten (ed.), *The Millennium Book, A History of Orangeism in County Armagh*, 2000.

ACKNOWLEDGEMENTS

For their help during his research, the author wishes to thank David Cowan, Bertie Wright, Freddie Pearson, George McAdam, Gordon and Helen Lyttle, Sam Prescott, Tom Johnston, Mrs Emma Clarke, Alfred Johnston, Willie Johnston, Tom Singleton, James Whitten, Richard Whitten, Kenneth Lockhart, Alan Neill, Miss Sarah Rea, George Black, Roy Vogan, Robert Redpath, Greer Robinson, Carl Pinder, Shirley Anderson, Myrtle McGuinness, William Flack, Tommy Bothwell, Mrs Betina Harden of Tandragee Library, Joan Kinch of the Ulster Architectural Heritage Society, The Mitchell Library, Glasgow, and Tim Neal of the National Fairground Archive, Sheffield.

The publishers wish to thank Alfie Johnston for permission to reproduce the photographs on pages 31 and 33.

Cast in 1930 by the bellfounders Gillett and Johnstone of Croydon, this 16 hundredweight bell, dedicated to the memory of Maria and John Gracey and Hugh Rea, hangs, with two lesser bells, in the belfry of Mullavilly – 'the summit of the ancient tree' – Church, on the outskirts of Laurelvale. For such a large bell, preparing the brick, loam and sand core mould (giving the inner profile) is a major undertaking, before work starts on the outer mould with the inscription. Together their weight would have been twice that of the finished bell. Inverted and lowered into a pit in the foundry floor, the molten metal (thirteen parts copper to one part Cornish tin) is poured into the bell. Two weeks of natural cooling follows, before the casing is then removed and the highly specialised process of tuning is carried out, where, to attain perfect tone, up to half a ton of metal is removed. What brought the name of Hugh Rea, a farmer from Lisavague, who died in 1923 aged 59 years, together with those of the Graceys, possibly of Ballymore, could not be ascertained.

Viewed from Black's Lane, there is justification for George Bassett's opinion, given in *The Book of County Armagh*, that Tandragee, 'with its back to the wind', 'compares favourably with the most beautifully situated towns in Ireland'. By the time of this Napier photograph, taken twenty years later, little would have changed. In the far left foreground, to the left of Sinton's Mill chimney, stands the Presbyterian Church and its manse, with the castle on the skyline above. In the town itself the line of Mill Street, Market Street and the Square clearly wend their way up to the trees and the Church of Ireland tower in Church Street (which can just be seen above the trees), while the terraced houses in Montagu Street are to the right. The principal town in the parish of Ballymore, Tandragee, or 'Tanrygee' as it was once known, dates from 1619 when James I granted 300 acres of land to build a corporate town. Contemporary grants (each of 300 acres) went to Armagh, Mount Norris and Claremount. Surrounded by arable land growing oats, potatoes and flax, a market was established for linen, flax, grain and cattle, and in 1824 a flour and corn mill was built – a precursor to the linen mill – harnessing the power of the River Cusher.

Tandragee's ornately decorated 'Coronation Lamp', bearing the inscription 'E.R. 1902', was erected in the Square to celebrate the coronation of King Edward VII on 9 August 1902. It was probably paid for by the Duke of Manchester on whose estate the town stands. The boy on the plinth is holding up the commemorative medallion given to schoolchildren throughout the kingdom to mark this event. The lamp became a traffic hazard in later years and was moved to the junction of Portadown Road and Ballymore Road. Also in this photograph, immediately behind the lamp, are the premises of John O'Hare the baker and Thomas Harvey the spirit dealer.

A view of Market Street, just below the Square. On the right is the Manchester Arms, named for the feudal landlords, the Dukes of Manchester (the family name was also celebrated by the Mandeville Arms), while on the opposite side of the road are the premises of Miss Coburn, the haberdasher. James Wallace of the Manchester Arms was also a timber and iron merchant. The boy with the tennis racquet gives credence to George Bassett's report that Tandragee had a thirty-member tennis club, founded in 1878 with two grass courts in the castle grounds. The annual subscription was 7s 6d.

To announce their arrival in town in 1905, a performer from Bosco's Circus leads the promotional parade up Market Street by walking on a large ball. Formed in the 1870s by Irving Bosco, an aerial trapeze artist, the earliest known venue for Bosco's Royal Circus was Newcastle-upon-Tyne in 1880–81. At the turn of the century it toured Britain with a lantern slide show and newsreels from the Boer War. In 1907 Bosco joined Harry Poole (stage name 'Zanlo') and, until Bosco's death in 1911, they toured Ireland as Poole and Bosco's Electric Coliseum, a combined circus and cinema.

A view of Mill Street, leading down to Sinton's Mill. From the newspaper flysheets outside Mrs Hughes' grocer's and bookseller's, we can see that Home Rule was in the news. Two doors down, Miss McCudden was also a grocer. Although Sinton became the town's major employer, the street's name actually derives from the corn and flour mill which was established in the town in the 1820s by John Creery of Tullyhugh and employed sixteen men. By the early twentieth century it was owned by Thomas H. White & Co.

Standing on Glebehill Road, on the banks of the River Cusher, was Thomas Sinton & Sons' flax spinning and linen yarn manufacturing mill, Sintonville. It was a corn mill until 1865 when James Rowlie and Robert Davis of the Tandragee Flax Spinning Company bought and converted it to spinning. Within six years Rowlie and Davis were bankrupt and Sinton, who had spinning mills at Laurelvale and Killyleigh, took over. Its 600 employees produced heavy duty yarn. After a period of diminishing production the mill finally closed in the early 1990s and there are now plans to redevelop it as a centre for small businesses.

Church Street has changed little since William Napier took this photograph from the Square in the early twentieth century – catching two of the Jubilee Lamp bollards on the right. Built in the nineteenth century by the Manchester family, the walkway or 'Mall' on the left was designed to keep members of the family off the muddy street on their walk to church. Today it is a favourite viewpoint for parades and marches.

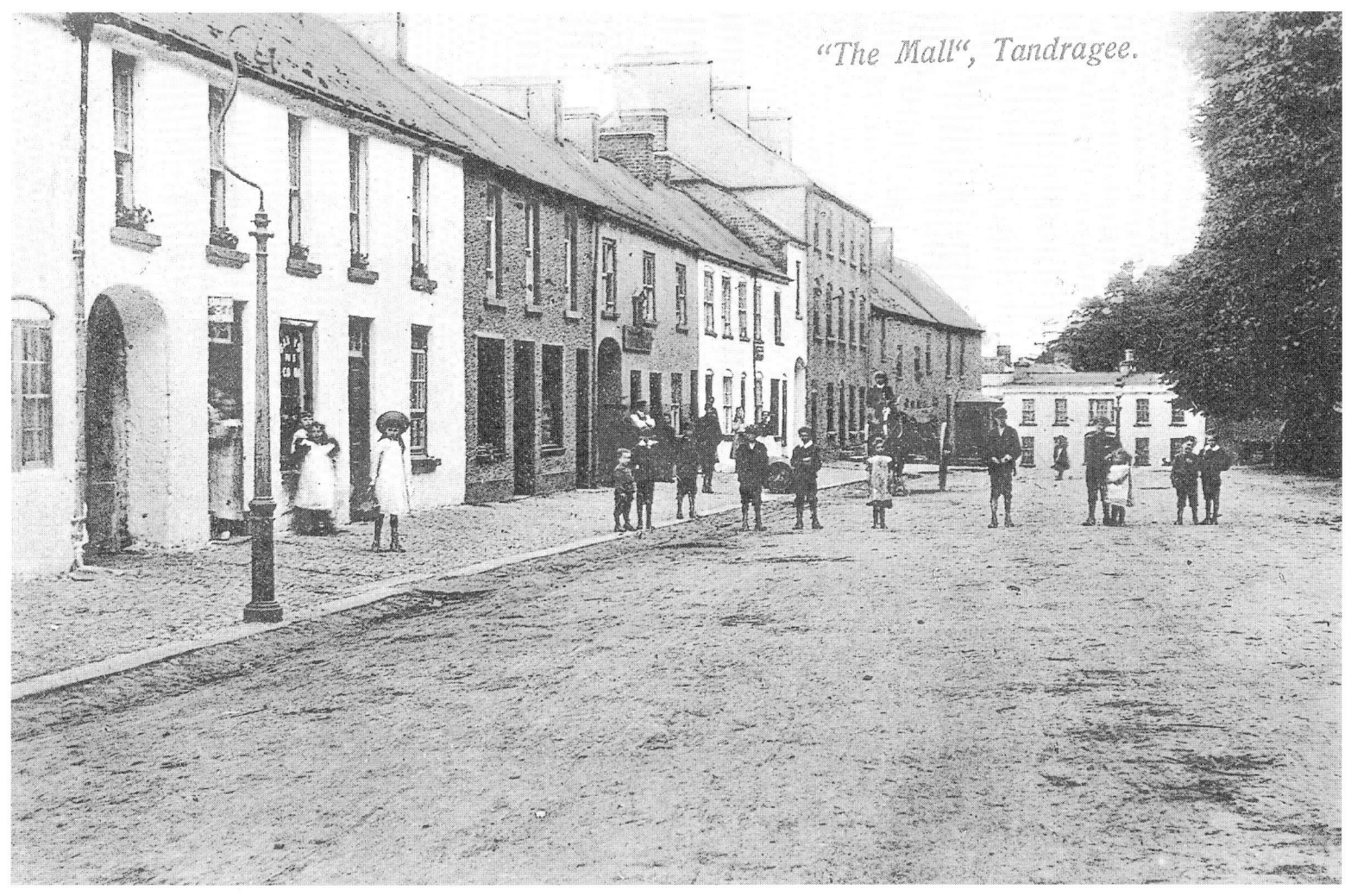

Looking back along Church Street towards the Square, 1907. The street is named after Tandragee Church, a plain rectangular building and tower, which stands out of view to the right. Dating from 1622, it was rebuilt in 1812 at a cost of £2,300, of which Lady Mandeville of the Manchester family donated £700.

Tandragee Masonic Hall on Church Street, photographed in 1915. Following a dispute at the Loughbrickland lodge in 1828, a number of the brethren broke away and formed Lodge No. 105 at Tandragee. In the spring of 1874 a building fund was opened and on 13 August that year the foundation stone was laid. With the site sloping down from the roadside, the single storey front hides the fact that the building is a double storey to the rear, where a three apartment ground floor caretaker's house was incorporated. Tommy Bothwell, who lived there with his wife Lucinda, was the last caretaker from 1955 until the 1970s. In 1992 the building was extended to the corner of Montagu Street.

Dating from the nineteenth century, Montagu Street housed workers from the Manchester estate. The view has changed since this photograph was taken in 1909 as the house on the left has since been demolished for road development and the Masonic hall now extends in from the right to the corner of the field.

On the east bank of the Newry Canal, Tandragee Harbour stretched along either side of the bridge carrying the road to Gilford. Along the canal, horse-drawn barges, carrying 80 to 90 tons, brought coal from Newry for Sinton's mills at Tandragee and Laurelvale. The coal was shovelled into one hundredweight creels which were hoisted by derricks into contracted farmers' carts; the farmers were paid 1s 6d per ton to Tandragee and 2s 6d to Laurelvale. The quayside storage buildings belonged to James Whiteside, the Tandragee coal merchant of Market Street, and the white house, demolished around 1980, was home to Anna Neil. The towpath ran along the left bank to the bridge where the rising wall allowed the tow rope to follow the horse onto the roadway. There it was unhitched as the barge passed underneath. These horses had a life expectancy of around eighteen months. The bridge was rebuilt and widened in the early 1990s.

Photographed in 1910, this Sharp Stewart B class 0-6-0, No. 62 'Tyrone', built in 1877 and in service until 1930, stands at the station variously known as 'Madden Bridge' or 'Tandragee and Gilford' or, from 1894, simply 'Tandragee'. The station was actually 1.3 miles from the village; such was the influence of nineteenth century landowners – in this case the Duke of Manchester – in keeping the railway off their land, that many stations were built far from the communities they served. The line and station at Tandragee were opened by the Dublin and Belfast Junction Railway in 1852 and its main business was the haulage of coal and provisions. This view, taken from the road bridge over the line, shows the service roads on each side of the track, the main station building, the stationmaster's house, and his vegetable garden. The station was closed on 4 January 1965 and the buildings have since been demolished.

A later view of the station, by which time a footbridge had been built. Fatalities were previously not uncommon. On the right is the four bedroom – each with a service bell – Madden Inn (now a private dwelling) which for many years was run by Joseph Hall from Co. Tyrone. George Davison of the Temperance Hotel and posting house in Market Street provided passenger transport to Tandragee.

Built in the 1830s by George Montagu, sixth Duke of Manchester (1799–1855), Tandragee Castle was described by George Bassett as a 'Gothic Extravaganza'. From the eleventh century until the time of the Plantation it was an O'Hanlon stronghold, but was then granted to Sir Oliver St John. The O'Hanlons later re-took and destroyed it. It later came to the Sparrow family, and by marriage to the Mandevilles, and it was the sixth Duke of Manchester who undertook the building of the present castle between 1830 and 1838. Using greywacke stone quarried at Tullyhugh, it was built in the Elizabethan style. The Manchesters kept ownership until 1939, when it was requisitioned by the War Department as a base for American forces. In 1955 local businessman Thomas Hutchinson bought the castle and its 200 acres and within a year was producing from it 5,000 packets of potato crisps per week. Today his company, now Tayto (NI) Ltd, employs over 320 people, producing approximately 8 million packets per week.

A steam-driven traction engine and threshing machine, belonging to the contractor T. Collen of Bloomhill, at work on a farm near Tandragee. By 1904 Collen had moved on to Ballynock, although he was still in the business of 'hauling, threshing, stone-breaking and hay-pressing – all done at shortest notice'. Machines such as these saw the end of the labour-intensive days of hand reaping, flailing and winnowing. The traction engine would have arrived at the farm with the thresher on tow and the drive belt would have then been unpacked and linked up to the thresher while the driver got the engine's fire going. The relatively large outlay required for farmers to purchase their own machinery meant good business and a hectic harvest time for Collen and his men.

Church Street, Poyntzpass, with Ward and Rafferty's garage on the left and the tower of Acton Parish Church in the background. Built in 1793, the church takes its name from the village of Iron Acton in Gloucestershire which was the home of Sir Charles Poyntz, who arrived with the English army in the early seventeenth century. What had been Fenwick's Pass, a strategic strong point on the route across Ulster, now became Poyntzpass. However, it was only with the arrival of Alexander Thomas Stewart, a descendant of Poyntz, in the late eighteenth century, that a settlement of any importance was founded. While researching the *Ordnance Survey Memoir* in January 1838, J. Hill Williams counted ninety-three houses and twenty-two mud cabins in the community.

A view of the Square – which from the 1880s was the site of a Friday market for fowl, eggs and butter – looking towards Meeting Street. The Northern Bank on the left has been gone for many years past, as has Mickey Waddell's fishing tackle shop and Jim O'Loughlin's grocer shop on the corner. Behind the parked car stood Morrow's shoe shop and the original post office; renovation work in the early 1990s revealed interior walls of turf and mortar which were replaced for fire safety.

Until the 1930s, some twenty years after this photograph was taken, Miss Lancaster, who occupied the two storey house (with the potato drills), was the Poyntzpass area Inspector of Nurses. Beyond is St Joseph's Church, built around 1794 on ground leased at one shilling and one penny per annum from Alexander Thomas Stewart, who was then developing the village. Mentioned in the 1837 *Ordnance Survey Memoirs*, it could accommodate 500 people. Despite extensive renovations in 1907, 1958 and 1988, it retains its eighteenth century appearance and charm.

The opening of the Dublin and Belfast Junction Railway line in 1852 brought Poyntzpass into the new age of steam and what previously may have been called Canal Street became Railway Street.

Standing with a goods train at Poyntzpass Station is locomotive No. 29, 'Enniskillen', an 0-6-0 AL class which was built at Dundalk by the Great Northern Railway in 1895. Poyntzpass was the most southerly of the three small stations built between Portadown and Goraghwood when the Dublin and Belfast Junction Railway built its single line from Portadown to Drogheda in 1852 (the others being Scarva and Tandragee). It became a double line in 1862. The station closed in 1965 but reopened as a commuter halt in 1984.

A party of Edwardian gentlemen arrive by carriage at the Railway Hotel, then run by Joseph Searight who also operated the adjoining Scotch & Wigan Coal Yard. The Newry Canal opened in the 1740s, but the earliest record of these buildings dates from 1800. The 'humpback' bridge, shown here, was rebuilt in the early 1950s.

This 1917 photograph of Joseph Searight's premises by the canal, with perhaps him and his sons on the canal bank, shows the gable end of the Railway Hotel and his wine and spirit stores. The Belfast and Ulster Directory of 1904 lists H. Searight of the Cyclists Bar, Joseph Searight of the Railway Hotel and Mrs Searight, a draper. In the Scotch & Wigan Coal Yard building, and a similar one out of view to the right, he stored off-loaded coal and timber awaiting distribution. In the 1920s the Searights sold out to John Kelly, the Newry and Warrenpoint coal merchant. Kelly then sold the business in 1934 to Henry R. Clarke, whose family still own it.

Poyntzpass Harbour, on the west side of the canal, with the path leading to the bridge and the lock-keeper's house on the corner of Railway Street. The signal box at the level crossing can be seen between the arms of the derrick. The moored lighter had probably brought logs from Newry. The old gentleman sitting with the girls may have been the lock-keeper William Moody.

A later view of the harbour from the 1920s. By then more and more of the canal's traffic had been lost to the railway and the derrick had gone. The gentleman on the lock arm may have been one of William Moody's sons. Like their father, both Thomas and James were carpenters and also held the post of lock-keeper, living in the house by the bridge.

A woman and two children pose by the wall rounding into Markethill's Newry Street around 1910. The premises up the left side of Main Street were J. Mallagh the grocer, J. Maguire's Railway Hotel, Mrs Robinson's Imperial Bar, with the sign above the door (she also sold agricultural implements), the Misses Kerr, one a dressmaker and the other a confectioner, George Armstrong, teacher, Robert Small the draper, Mrs Smith's Central Bar, William Taylor the draper, Miss Allen, a teacher, and the Morgans, who had a butcher's shop and the public house on the Keady Street corner.

Contemporary with the previous photograph, this view shows the opposite view of the lower end of Main Street, down to the Market. Down the left side of the street local people have recalled that there were once the premises of J. Adams the carpenter, James Stockdale the saddler, Miss McParland who sold Delfware, and the houses of Miss McKee, Nurse Hutton, J. Irvin the teacher and John Swann who was a coachman at Gosford Castle. There was also the police barracks with its arch, and the home of Sergeant Walshman, T. Wilson the tailor, J. Glasey's lodging house and Mrs Robinson's Corner Bar. Coming up on the opposite side was Edwards' the grocer, James Johnston the hairdresser, standing on his step with his arms folded, Miss Sampson the Delfware seller and Edwards' post office.

Opened in 1864, Markethill railway station was the Newry and Armagh Railway Company's principal station on the Goraghwood – Armagh line and was midway between these two towns. Financial and physical problems thwarted their initial hopes of taking the line to Enniskillen and of building a second platform. Closed for a rail strike in 1933, the Markethill to Armagh line never reopened and the one to Goraghwood closed in 1955. The main commodity on the line was Newry coal. The staff and the signalbox are long gone, but the main station building survives as a dwellinghouse.

Photographed from Greenpark Avenue around 1910, this view across the railway lines and the sidings, with their flat and open G.N.R. wagons, shows the First Presbyterian Church on Fairgreen Road. Founded in 1609, the congregation had used a cottage as a meeting house before this building was put up in 1899–1900.

MULLABRACK CHURCH AND SCHOOL, MARKETHILL.

It is not possible to date the founding of St James's Church at Mullabrack. Dating from at least the late sixteenth century it was 'not wholly rebuilt' in 1609, was then partially destroyed in the 1641 Rebellion, and again rebuilt by 1693. On the left was the primary school, with the infant school out of shot to the right of the gateway. Thought to date from 1821, both schools were closed in 1986 and the pupils transferred to the new school at Hamiltonsbawn. The building in the photograph now serves the church as a hall.

Pupils of Mullabrack Primary School line up for their annual photograph in the late 1930s. They are: *back row* (left to right) – G. Edwards, N. Scott, W. Singleton, J. Callaghan, S. Cromwell, W. Scott, ? Wallace, M. Edwards, I. Adams, F. Singleton, S. Murray, H. McMullan; *third row* – E. Martin, J. Bell, J. McMurray, W. Wallace, M. Parkes, B. Bell, E. Cromwell, M. McMurray, M. Magill, M. McHugh, E. McHugh, I. Edwards, M. McMurray, J. McMullan, D. McClean; *second row* – J. McStay, T. McKew, J. Spence, J. McKew, M. McHugh, G. McHugh, M. McClean, J. McMullan, S. Wilson, P. Spence, L. Spence, M. McMullan, A. Martin, L. McKew, M. Irvin, M. Swann, John Adam, J. McStay; *front row* – J. Cromwell, Alfie Johnston, F. Willis, W. Spence.

MARKETHILL

The original manor house at Markethill, put up in 1617 by Sir Archibald Acheson, first Baronet of Gosford, was destroyed in the 1641 Rebellion. Its replacement was lost to a fire and this 'Norman Revival' style building, known as Gosford Castle, was commissioned in 1819 by Archibald Acheson, second Earl of Gosford (1806–1864), with funding from the family of his wife, Mary Sparrow. They were later estranged. An 1837 report describes it as, 'a sumptuous and stately structure . . . of Mullaglass granite'. With over 150 rooms it was reckoned to be the largest pile in Ireland. Falling on hard times, the fifth Earl, Sir Archibald Charles Montagu Brabazon Acheson (1887–1954), was forced to vacate the castle in 1921. During the Second World War it was commandeered and used as an army base and prisoner of war camp. The Department of Agriculture's purchase in 1958 launched the successful Gosford Forest Park, but the castle has been less fortunate. In 1980 a consortium was granted a ninety-nine year lease and given five years to return it to its former glory. They failed. Currently, there are plans to convert it into twenty-four flats.

The gamekeeper's cottage at the entrance to Gosford Castle from the Markethill to Tandragee road. Thought to date from around 1700, careful maintenance and expert restoration over the years have preserved this unique house. The exact identities of the trio in this photograph, which dates from around 1900, are unknown, but it is likely that they are the gamekeeper and his wife, with Lady Louisa Augusta Beatrice Montagu, wife of the fourth Earl of Gosford, Sir Archibald Brabazon Sparrow Acheson (1841–1922).

In *The Book of County Armagh*, George Bassett wrote that Glenanne 'is one of the prettiest villages in the county'. The village was created to house the workers of George Gray & Sons' linen mill. The firm also owned the co-operative store on the left and the sixty or so houses in the village.

The Upper Mills at Glenanne, seen here around 1925, date back to 1818 when William Atkinson established a cotton spinning and weaving mill. The whole property, including the village and bleach greens, extended to 250 acres. George Gray acquired the business in the early 1840s, converting to linen manufacture in the 1850s. Water from Shaw's Lake ran through six breast wheels and a Macadam turbine to power 316 looms. In the late nineteenth century the mill was employing 400 workers. Today, the premises are shared between Glenanne Jacquard, the clothing manufacturer, and the poultry and egg producer, Johnstons of Mountnorris.

Richhill's history dates to the Plantation Scheme of 1610, when the manor lands of Mullaleish and Legacorry were given to Sir Francis Sacheverell of Ravesby in Nottinghamshire. The original name, Legacorry, became Richardson's Hill and this was later abbreviated to Richhill. In 1814 the town's population was 734, and with 161 houses it had six more than Portadown. However, the coming of the railway in 1848 and the new Armagh to Belfast road, via Portadown (today's A3), brought decline to Richhill. This view shows Main Street (once named Broad Street) as it was in 1909.

THE CHURCH, RICHHILL, CO ARMAGH.

The children's clothing in this view of Richhill's Square and St Matthew's Church also dates this photogragh to around the same era. The church building was erected in 1753 when William Richardson of 'the Castle' built it to house Richhill's linen market, but in a later period of decline (from a peak weekly turnover of £1,500) it was converted to a chapel of ease, serving Armagh. The *Ordnance Survey Memoirs* report that it cost £620 to convert. It was consecrated as St Matthew's Church on 14 September 1837.

The tower of St Matthew's Church was added at a cost of £300 and consecrated on Empire Day, Saturday, 24 May 1913. The clock, a commemorative gift from the Rountree family, and the tower's ivy coat came later. Photographed on a summer's morning in 1916, the presence of an Inglis baker's van is the only sign of activity.

A view of Irish Street, looking to the Square and the trees in the grounds of Richhill Castle. Built in 1610 by Sir Francis Sacheverell, the original castle was rebuilt in the 1660s by Major Edward Richardson, who had married Sacheverell's granddaughter Anne. A two storey house with attics, a number of owners have passed through over the years, including Dolly Monroe, 'The Star of County Down', and the government who, in 1936, moved the entrance gates to Hillsborough Castle.

John Jackson's grocery and hardware store stood at the end of Tandragee Street, where the road divides for Portadown to the left and Mullaleish to the right. Through his ownership of seven acres of land (the farm buildings to the right were also his), he appears in the Armagh Landowners List of 1876, and is mentioned as a shop owner in Bassett's *The Book of County Armagh*. His ownership was also noted in the Belfast and Ulster Directory of 1904. However, within a few years of this photograph the farm and the shop were bought by Joney Troughton, and, while the farm survives, many years later the shop, the house and the outbuildings were demolished for a new housing development.

Coming to a green field site, a mile and a half from Tandragee, in the early 1850s, Thomas Sinton built this weaving mill and the village of Laurelvale around it. Powered by two 180 horsepower steam engines, the mill's 350 looms employed a work force of 700 to produce superior heavy linens and sheetings. Sinton died in 1887 and was followed in the business by his sons. At the time of this photograph, taken in 1907, the mill was owned by the Cochrane family, but by the late 1930s ownership had passed to Hoffman the ball bearing manufacturer. The mill has since been demolished and its site is vacant.

This Edwardian photograph shows the top of Main Street, or 'Co-hill', where the line of houses ends with the co-operative general store, founded by Thomas Sinton.

The houses of Quality Hill, each with a parlour and two bedrooms, were built for the overseers and foremen of the mill. It was Thomas Sinton's choice that each had a green front door, through which he had the habit of appearing – unannounced – on inspection visits. There are a lot fewer children about today!

The two storey, three bedroom houses on Coronation Row were designed for workers with larger families and consisted of a parlour and kitchen on the ground floor and had three bedrooms upstairs.

The Village, Loughgall.

Samuel Fox's general store lives on as a Centra shop, Main Street having altered little in the past century. The house on the left was the headmaster's, fronting the Cope family sponsored school behind, followed by the R.I.C. barracks and the Ensor Masonic Hall (built in 1902) as the road leads out to Moore's Dairy at the far end. Loughgall's history dates back to the ninth century, although it wasn't until the late 1600s that the village grew around the manor estate established at that time by Sir Anthony Cope of Hanwell, Oxfordshire (the estate remained in the family until it was purchased by the Ministry of Agriculture in 1947). On 21 September 1795, following the Battle of the Diamond, the first Orange warrant was signed in James Sloan's house, opposite the courthouse. Part of the house now holds the Orange Museum.

Looking north along Main Street, the courthouse of 1776 stands out in the centre. The court, which operated until the 1930s, was on the upper floor, while the open, arched, ground floor held the market. Set in the 'Garden of Ireland', with acre upon acre of apple orchards, Loughgall's September market days were very busy. Now huge lorries carry the apples through the village on their way to processing plants.

In 1926 James Whitten of the general store at Clare, or more correctly Old Clare, commissioned the postcard producer Coon of Letterkenny and Moira to photograph these, his two premises on the junction of Old Clare Road and Cloghoge Road. The photographer's motorcycle and sidecar stand by the village pump. David Stuart Whitten (1872–1925) built the shop and house on the right in 1890, but around 1908 he emigrated to America, leaving the business to his brother, James (1870–1946) who was a stone mason from Tandragee. David served with the Mexican Army and later was killed falling from a horse in western Canada. In 1925–26 James built the premises on the left corner for drapery, grocery, hardware and agricultural supplies, and the family ran this side of their business until 1963 when it was rented to the carpet supplier Colin Robinson. In the 1980s it fell vacant and was demolished in August 2002. Planning permission has been granted for housing. The group crossing the junction would have been coming from a funeral at the Reformed Presbyterian Church on Cloghoge Road.

The Whitten family, photographed in the summer of 1915 with local farmer's wives, on the right, who would have been making their weekly deliveries of eggs and butter. In the group at the left-hand doorway, giving access to the house, are Annie Whitten (1906–1989) and her sister Meta (1907–1990). To the left of the centre doorway, giving access to the main shop, Mrs Alice Jane Whitten (1874–1941) stands with her youngest, James William Whitten (1915–), in her arms and her daughter Eileen (1912–) at her side. The annexe to the right was for drapery and boots and shoes. It was demolished in 1958. The business traded until 1990 when the main building was converted into living accommodation.